Black carpenter ants crawl along a log.

THE WORLD OF
ANTS

HOW THEY LIVE, WORK, AND COMMUNICATE WITHIN THEIR COLONIES

by G. COLLINS WHEAT

Illustrated with photographs
Drawings by ERIC MOSE

REVISED EDITION 1961

GOLDEN PRESS NEW YORK

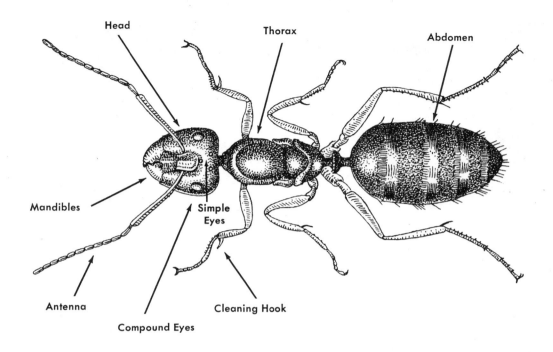

Head   Thorax   Abdomen

Mandibles   Simple Eyes

Antenna   Cleaning Hook

Compound Eyes

This diagram shows a dorsal view of an ant.

What Is an Ant?

The ant is an insect, and insects are invertebrate animals, which means that they have no backbone. Instead of an inside skeleton of bone, most insects have outside skeletons — tough, shiny coverings containing a substance called chitin. Even the legs of insects are covered with this armor, and are jointed like the legs of a crab.

Harvester ants store seeds and grain in special chambers in their nests.

An insect has two body sections and a head; the first section, where the legs and wings are connected, is the thorax; and the second section is the abdomen, or stomach. Insects have six legs, and some, but not all, have wings.

Creatures that make up the class called "insect" account for four-fifths of all the animals in the world. There are nearly a million insect species known, and many more are undiscovered. Over 6,000 ant species have been described.

7

The wasp and the bee are both members of the order called Hymenoptera.

Ants, Bees, and Wasps

The insect class, like other classes of animals, is divided into orders. An order is a group of animals that are related to each other, and have much in common.

Ants, bees, and wasps are all related, and are placed in the order called *Hymenoptera*. This is a Greek word meaning "membrane wings," or wings that are thin and transparent. The ant's body is very much like that of the bee or the wasp, but all bees have wings, and only male ants and young females have wings. This is an important difference between these cousins of the *Hymenoptera*. In other ways, the ants and the bees are very much alike. The *Hymenoptera* is considered the most advanced of all the insect orders, and contains the greatest number of social members living in communities rather than alone.

The ant has a body similar to those of the wasp and bee, its Hymenoptera *relatives.*

Daceton *ant*

Imported fire ant

The Ant's Head

The ant's head contains a small brain, and compound eyes which are made of many small lenses. With this kind of eye, the ant can see moving objects more easily than objects which stand still. Compound eyes do not move in sockets, but are fixed. Some ants can see better than others, and some ants, like the driver ants of Africa, are blind.

The mandibles, or jaws, of an ant are powerful and are used to cut up food and to carry materials for nests. Sharp jaws can be deadly weapons in ant wars. Unlike our own, ant jaws move sideways.

Atta *ant*

Eciton *army ant*

9

Attached to the head of an ant are its feelers, or antennae. The ant uses its antennae to communicate with other ants and to taste and feel different objects. With its sensitive antennae, the ant examines a particle of food on all sides, and can discover what it is like before putting it in its mouth. Antennae are so necessary that when they are cut off in warfare, the ant soon dies.

Ants never seem to get lost, going back and forth between their nests and food sources. When an ant finds food, it leaves an odor trail behind it. In some species, tiny drops of liquid are trailed from the tip of the abdomen as the ant hurries back to the nest. At home, other ants are alerted by the distinctive movements and the smell of the scent. They follow the scent trail to the food. Each ant colony has its own odor, and ants are not easily confused by the trails of other colonies. Once ant trails are established, the ants move along them quickly, their antennae tapping like canes.

Ants use their antennae for other purposes. One ant may stroke another, which means that it wishes to be fed. Some beetles and aphids also respond to gentle stroking, and squeeze out sweet body juices, a favorite ant food.

Ants, busy at their labors, will often pause to clean their antennae. To do this, they pull each antenna through a tiny hook in one of the joints of their forelegs. The hooks have tiny comb-like ridges on them and they keep the antennae free from dust and dirt.

Ants use their antennae to communicate with each other.

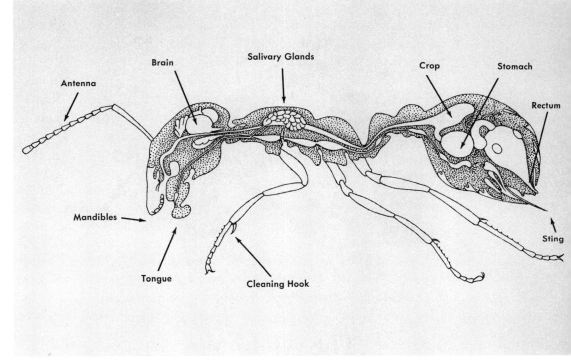

A cross section shows an ant's internal organs.

The Thorax

The thorax, or chest section, of the ant contains the heart and also the salivary glands for food digestion. Ant saliva is used to break down starch foods into sugar.

All six legs of the ant are connected to the thorax. The winged males and young females also have wing muscles in the thorax. The thorax of the queen is greatly enlarged, since she too, at one time, had wings.

The ant's body has no arteries or veins. The heart pumps the colorless blood freely through the hollow body sections. The blood supplies the ant's organs with oxygen. Ants can be active only in warm weather for their body temperature is regulated by surrounding conditions. During cold weather ants do not die but merely become sluggish and suspend their normal activities. The members of an ant colony cluster together in thousands around their valuable queen, keeping her warm.

One Formica *ant feeds another by bringing up food from its crop.*

The Abdomen

Perhaps the most unusual part of the ant's body is its stomach. Actually, the ant has two separate stomachs. The larger one, called the crop, is like a social stomach because food is stored here for the benefit of other ants. Food passes first into this crop, and then, if the ant needs nourishment for its own body, the food must be pumped out of the crop and into the second stomach. When the workers return to the nest with crops full of food, they pump food out for the queens, the young ants, and any other ants who have remained at home. One ant feeds another by bringing up a drop of liquid which is transferred from mouth to mouth. Food in the social stomach is always in liquid form, such as honeydew, or the fluids sucked from insect bodies.

Ants do not have lungs, but they breathe air through special holes in the sides of the abdomen. Muscular action makes the abdomen stretch and contract like an accordion. Air is forced into the holes and through tubes into the body.

In many ants the abdomen contains a stinger. Some ants, like the bees, plunge their stingers into the bodies of their enemies or victims. Others squirt poison through special funnels. Most ant stings are not harmful to man, but some ants, like the fire ant, inflict extremely painful stings.

Prehistoric Ants

Nearly one hundred million years ago, in the early part of the Tertiary period, ants were already living on the earth. The bodies of ants have been found preserved in hardened resin, or amber. Certain forms of these early ants were almost exactly like the ants in our gardens and fields today. Ordinarily, animals change throughout their centuries on earth. The horse, for example, was once no larger than a fox. Then, after millions of years, the horse reached its present size. The earliest birds had teeth and simple wings. Modern birds

Early horses and birds were very different from their modern day counterparts, but there has been little change in the hardy ants since prehistoric times.

13

have no teeth and have highly developed wings. Such changes are known as animal evolution.

Some animals may change a great deal, others very little, and still others become extinct. Animals become extinct if they cannot adjust themselves to changing conditions. They become extinct if they cannot protect themselves against enemies, or get enough food, or provide for the safety of their young.

A study of the earth's long past shows us that geography and climate have changed greatly throughout time. The hot, steamy swamps of one hundred to two hundred million years ago enabled the dinosaurs to multiply, and this part of the Mesozoic era is known as "The

Dinosaurs became extinct when the climate and other conditions changed.

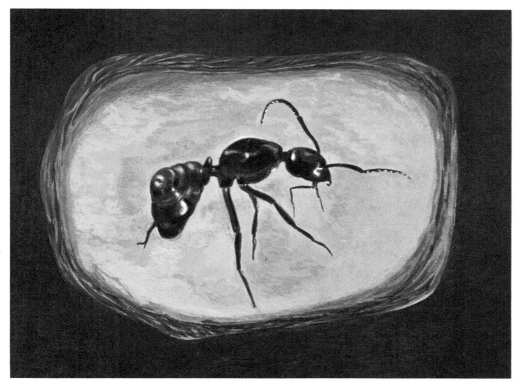

Early ants, trapped in resin, were preserved for millions of years.

Age of Dinosaurs." Yet dinosaurs became extinct before the next geologic era began. Because of climate changes, food supply of some species became inadequate, and perhaps the eggs and young of the dinosaurs were not protected from new land enemies. Whatever the causes, the dinosaurs died out.

Later, during the ice ages, the giant mammoths and mastodons roamed the frozen north. They became extinct about ten thousand years ago. Like the dinosaurs, they were unable to adjust to changing conditions. The large bodies of mammoths and mastodons are still dug out of glacier remains in the Arctic, the meat perfectly preserved.

But since the Mesozoic era until the present day, no earth changes have been severe enough to disturb the hardy ants. No enemies have been able to destroy them, and the ants have always been able to find food and shelter for their young. Like many other insects, the ants have multiplied so greatly in number that they can now be found in almost all parts of the earth. But most important of all, due to their long, steady period of evolution, the ants have had time to develop their remarkable instincts.

Animal Instinct

The term *instinct* is used by scientists to mean unlearned patterns of animal habits. It does not involve intelligence, thought, learning, or even memory. We marvel at the ants because they build complicated passages and rooms underground. We marvel at the way they make slaves of other ants, milk aphids for their honeydew, and even grow fungus for food. We compare the marching columns of army ant invaders with the armies of men. But the ants do not "reason" these things out; they simply do what their ancestor ants did before them, without thinking why. This ancestral habit, which all ants seem to have from birth, is known as instinct. In the following pages it will certainly seem as if the ants are the most intelligent of creatures, but it would be more correct for us to say that they have very highly developed instincts.

Leafcutter ants cultivate fungus for food by instinct, not thought.

Monarch butterfly chrysalis

Adult monarch and its caterpillar larva

The Egg, the Larva, and the Pupa

When we imagine what an ant looks like, we usually think of the adult only. We think of an active insect with six legs and a hard, jointed body. But the ant does not begin life looking like this. In becoming an adult, it goes through four transformations, or stages. Each stage is quite different from the one before.

Many insects grow up in separate stages. The butterfly begins life as a tiny egg. Next, the egg hatches into a caterpillar. Then the caterpillar becomes a chrysalis and finally breaks open to release a graceful butterfly with brightly colored wings.

The four stages of growth in the ant are similar. They are called the egg, the larva, the pupa, and the adult. The stages other than the adult one are rarely seen, except by careful insect watchers.

Adult imported fire ants

Larvae, pupae and adult fire ants

17

An ant worker carries a cluster of eggs in its jaws. It may be taking newly laid eggs from the queen to the nursery or moving eggs to safety deep in the nest.

These eggs of the housefly are long and thin, while ants' eggs are oval-shaped.

18

A Japanese beetle larva is a white grub.

EGG CLUSTERS

Ant eggs, sometimes laid in clusters, are white and oval-shaped, and so small that fifty of them, side by side, would measure only an inch. As soon as the eggs are laid by the queen ants, they are moved to nursery rooms in the nest where nursemaid worker ants look after them. The eggs are laid in the spring and summer, and within a period of weeks or months (depending on the type of ant), the eggs hatch into the second, or larval stage.

HUNGRY LARVAE

Larva is a Latin word meaning mask, and it is true that the larvae of many insects "mask" the future form of the adult. The ant larva resembles a small white grub and though it may grow as large as an adult ant, it has no eyes, legs, or antennae. It is just a soft, wriggling body with a mouth. It seems hard to believe that such a creature will someday become a fast-moving black ant.

The same transformation occurs in the larvae of other insects. The larva of the butterfly is called a caterpillar, the larva of the housefly is called a maggot, and the larva of the beetle is called a grub. They all resemble crawling worms,

The butterfly larva is a caterpillar.

These are larvae of the army ant.

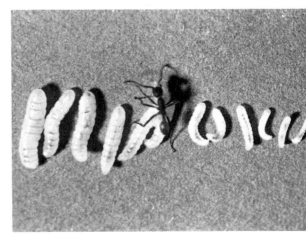

Imported fire ant pupae

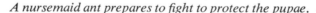

Adult imported fire ant

but when they finally grow up, one will be a frail yellow butterfly, one will be a black housefly, and one will be a shiny, iridescent green beetle!

Ant larvae are always hungry. In an ant colony, workers are kept busy for several weeks feeding the larvae. Then, suddenly, the larvae stop eating. They are ready to change into the next stage.

PUPAE

The third stage is known as the pupal stage. Now, for the first time, the faint outlines of the adult ant begin to ap-

A nursemaid ant prepares to fight to protect the pupae.

pear. The pupa is pale in color, with tiny legs and feelers tucked close to its body. The pupae, unlike the larvae, never eat. Instead, the pupal stage is a quiet period lasting several weeks or more. During this time, the various parts of the adult ant begin to take shape, though the pupa does not move. Some ant larvae, when they change into pupae, spin silk cocoons just like silk worms. Other pupae remain uncovered. In some countries, ant pupae are sold as "ant eggs." Used for bird and fish food, they are not really "eggs" but are the pupae wrapped in their silk cocoons.

YOUNG ADULTS

Finally, the pupa begins to move its legs and antennae. It is time for the birth of the young adult. The ants in the nest gather around, and if the pupa is struggling within its old pupal skin and cocoon, the older ants help it out. They tear with their jaws until the skin or the silk is ripped away. The young ant stands on its legs although it is still very weak. It is called a callow, and for a few days its body remains pale yellow. But soon the callow gains strength and turns dark like the other ants. Its body hardens, and it is ready to begin a lifetime of work, which may go on for about a month to several years. The callow needs no long learning period; it follows its instincts quickly, performing the complicated tasks that the older adults have been doing for years.

Wherever ants choose to make their homes—in logs, leaf nests, or in the ground—the young are carefully protected at all stages of growth. Worker ants risk their lives to save them. If an underground nest is flooded, the ants rescue their young at once. Crowded lines of excited ants will come streaming out of the nest holding eggs, larvae, and pupae in their jaws and will rush them to safer territory.

An ant worker carries a pupa.

A callow emerges from its cocoon.

21

The Queen of the Colony

The queen is the most important ant in the colony, for she is the mother of all the others. New ant colonies start from the eggs of one queen; but in compound nests, which may be fifty years old and contain thousands of ants, several queens will be laying eggs at the same time. Compound nests, like those formed by the Argentine ants, continue to grow in size as more and more queens lay eggs. In colonies with only one queen, or in young colonies, the death of the queen means the end of colony growth. No new ants can be born, and the remaining workers become less active, and soon die.

In active colonies, nursemaid ants wash the queen with their tongues, feed her the best foods, and move her freshly laid eggs to special nursery rooms. In the daytime, when the sun warms the surface of the ground, the eggs are placed in nurseries near the top of the nest. During the night, if the air turns cold, the eggs are moved again to deeper, warmer rooms. Much larger than the workers, the queen spends most of her life laying eggs, and some queens can lay eggs every few minutes.

Each queen begins life as a young, winged female. She does not have to help build the nest or gather and store

A winged female readies herself for her mating flight.

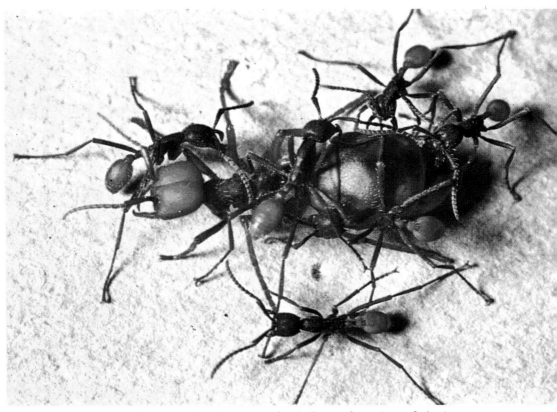

Army ant workers attend their queen, who is almost three times their size.

food. This labor is done entirely by the workers. In every colony there are a few winged males, or drones, who do not work either. It might be said that the winged ants are the royalty of the colony.

The royalty of the colony live in luxury until a special day comes along. This is the swarming day, the day on which the young winged males and females leave the nest and fly into the air, testing their wings for the first time. No one can predict just when this day will be, in spring, midsummer or late summer, but the ants seem to know by some inner signal. When swarming occurs, the flying ants are blown by the wind. Sometimes the wind scatters the ants for many miles, which is one reason ants of the same species are found over large areas.

On swarming day, all the ants become excited, and then suddenly the flight begins. Even ants without wings become so excited they run as fast as they can, and climb to the tops of grass stems and high stones, even into trees. They urge the winged ants to begin the flight. But, of course, only the winged royalty can take to the air.

On swarming day, winged males and females gather for the nuptial flight.

THE BIRTH OF A COLONY

High above the ground the winged males mate with the females. The males die quickly, but for each fertile female a new life is beginning. She drifts with the wind currents until she finally drops to earth. She may be a great distance from her old nest, and entirely alone, but she knows what to do. She seeks shelter by digging a hole in the ground or crawling under a stone. Then she seals herself underground, making herself a prisoner. She is ready to start laying her eggs.

As soon as she is settled, the young female bites or rubs off her wings. She will never fly again; she has become a true queen. Though she may live for

Winged female ants and pupae lie in the cells of the nest.

fifteen more years, she will never again go above ground.

The queen must wait many days, and sometimes as long as eight or nine months, before her first eggs will grow into useful ants. The first eggs are small, and the queen must eat some of them to stay alive. Another source of food is the queen's wing muscles. Since the wings are gone, the muscles in her thorax are useless. Little by little the muscles shrink, giving extra nourishment to the queen's body.

When the first eggs turn into larvae, the queen must feed them with saliva juices from her mouth. The queen must wait for her larvae to turn into pupae and finally into callows. The first ants born are small and weak. They may live only a short time, but they are strong enough to dig their way out of the queen's chamber and search for food. Once they begin to feed the queen, bringing down insect meat and honeydew from the sunlit world above, the queen is able to lay more and more eggs. Before long, the colony has healthy adult ants and is growing at a rapid rate. The young workers dig tunnels and carve new rooms, but the queen is still fed and cared for always.

A few of the queen's eggs grow into winged males and an even smaller number grow into winged females. By far the greatest number of eggs turn into worker ants. The workers are all wingless females. Also, since the workers are incomplete females, most can never lay eggs. It is this form of adult ant that we see most often.

Young winged ants

Carpenter ant workers

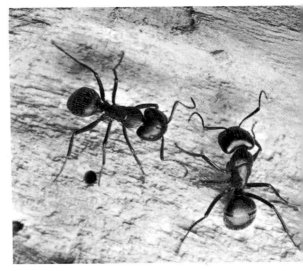

Mound of the imported fire ant   *Hole of the little black ant*

Ant Homes

Since ants live in almost all parts of the world, from the dry deserts to the damp tropics, it is easy to see why their homes must differ. In fact, some ants in the tropics have no homes at all. Nomadic, or wandering, ants merely form a living wall of workers around the queens and young ants.

CARPENTER ANTS

Where climates are cold, such as in northern forests, permanent shelters are necessary. Carpenter ants build in wood. With their strong jaws, they crush wood fibers and push the sawdust out of the tunnels. They bore across the grain into trees, and sometimes into the beams and foundations of houses. Rooms are hollowed out inside the wood, and the colony lives in a very secure home. Some wood ants have thick heads which are used as front doors. Entrances to the nests are the same size as the heads of the sentries, and when ant-heads block the openings, enemies cannot get inside. When workers return to the nests carrying food, they are admitted by the "janitors" only when the right taps from the antennae of the returning ants prove that they are friends.

A wood ant nest is usually built around a support, such as a tree stump or fence post.

26

The nest of the Colobopsis *ant has only one entrance. The door is plugged by the head of an ant who has retreated for a second to let this worker into the nest.*

There are many kinds of ants that live in the woods and use wood as their building material. Wood ants in European forests place pine needles and twigs above their mounds, so that the nests' upper rooms and tunnels will catch the low, warming rays of sunshine. Another type of wood ant uses rotten wood to form nests which hang from trees.

FLOWER-BALL HOMES

Certain ants from South America build flower-ball homes. In the rain forests, where floods and damp grounds

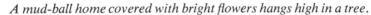

A mud-ball home covered with bright flowers hangs high in a tree.

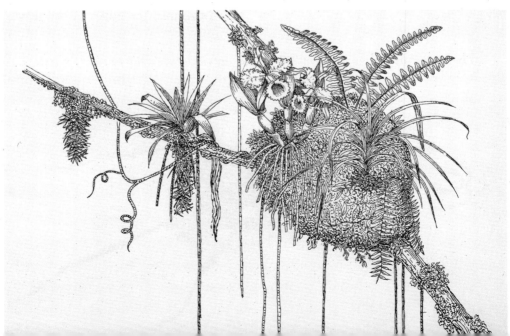

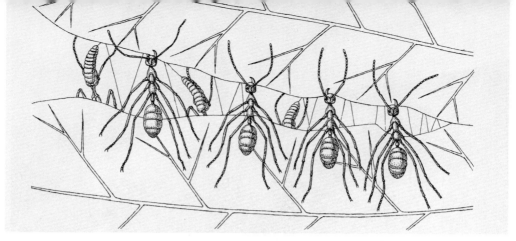

Weaver ants use the silk of their larvae to stitch leaves together.

are usual, these ants gather mud and carry it high into the trees. The mud is placed on a branch, each worker adding a mouthful at a time, until a large ball is formed. The mud ball may be as wide as eight inches, with rooms and tunnels inside. It is thought that flower seeds are carried up the tree by the ants and planted in the mud ball. After a while, the seeds sprout in the mud. The mud ball blooms with flowers, and the flower roots hold the nest together. Even during heavy tropical rainstorms, the flower-ball nest does not wash away.

WEAVER ANTS

Still other ants live in homes made of leaves. These weaver ants live in the tropics, and in some parts of Asia. The weaver ants select suitable leaves and pull the edges together with their jaws. Then, a remarkable event takes place. The young larvae of the weaver ants, who are able to spin silk for their co-coons, are held in the jaws of a second group of adult workers. The larvae give up strands of silk from their bodies and the workers "weave" the strands back and forth until the edges of the leaves

The spiny Polyrhachis *ant from Borneo also uses its larvae's silk to build its nest.*

The leaf-cutting Atta *ants burrow deep into the ground to carve out their rooms.*

are sewn together. This is one of the few examples in the animal kingdom of creatures using tools to do their work.

In China, the nests of weaver ants are cut down by farmers and hung in fruit trees. The weaver ants do no harm to the trees, but, since they are warlike ants, they drive off injurious insect pests.

HOMES UNDERGROUND

Most ants live underground, especially the types of ants common to our country. The Argentine ant, for example, may construct nests with many passages running below the surface of the earth. As we shall see, the *Atta* ants are even more energetic diggers. Their nests cover great areas and extend twenty feet or more into the ground. Ants such as the Chilean desert ant, which lives in dry areas, burrow deeply into the sand to escape the hot sun.

Ants pile dirt around their nest openings to form mounds, which vary in height from a few inches to mounds of soil several feet high. Other ants enter nests by small, well-concealed holes. In any case, the rooms below ground serve as food storage areas, nurseries, queen chambers, and rooms for the larvae to spin their cocoons. Ants are very neat, and remove their dead from the nest. Some place the bodies of dead ants in special areas set aside as "cemeteries."

Warring Ants

Almost all ant colonies are ready to wage war against neighboring colonies. Their purpose may be to enlarge their territory, to obtain food, or to capture slaves. The stronger ants take the offensive using several powerful weapons — agility, a stinger, and sharp jaws with which they bite and pierce the victim or saw off its head and legs. Some ants, like the *Formicinae*, can squirt a poison which causes temporary paralysis or death. The weaker ants must depend on a fast escape, a tough skin or playing dead to defend themselves.

The domination of the Argentine ants in this country has come about partly through their ability to drive away other species. The Argentines are very capable fighters. Some ants attack singly and without caution, rushing blindly at their enemies, but the Argentines work together. They attack in masses and surround a single enemy. Legs and antennae are chopped off quickly, and heads chewed through. Even against larger opponents like the wood ants, the Argentines are almost always the victors.

In this fight, one ant has seized the antennae of the other in its jaws.

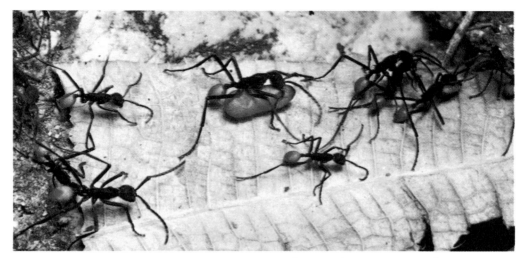

Army ants, one of which is carrying a pupa here, make no permanent homes.

The Army Ants

Army ants in tropical regions make no permanent homes. They bunch together in huge armies and march off to war, destroying and devouring every living creature in their path. And they do actually march. Long columns are formed, with the strongest soldier ants on the flanks, and the smaller ants on the inside. In the center of the army march the queen and the workers carrying the young. Even the hundreds of eggs and larvae are transported, the long-legged army ants carrying the large pupa cocoons beneath them.

The marching columns of the *Eciton,* the legionary ants of South America, may be hundreds of feet long and about one foot wide. The soldiers march close together, their bodies touching, and such a murderous carpet of ants may number even into the millions.

Some ants are omnivorous, meaning that they can eat all types of food, but army ants are carnivorous, which means meat-eating only. No animal is safe in the path of the drivers, as they are sometimes called. With their enormous jaws, sometimes half the length of their bodies, army ants can kill and devour all sorts of small animals. They can even destroy larger animals, such as rabbits and pythons, if these are injured, or are trapped in cages. A marching column of army ants has a strong unpleasant odor from bits of meat they carry with them.

The army ants leave nothing but the bones. Even rats and mice are not safe in their underground holes. Perhaps the

Army ants make stringlike bridges of their bodies in order to overcome obstacles.

best that can be said for the army ants is that during their marches, they may rid the area of rodent and insect pests.

Water does not have to be a barrier to the army ants. Small streams of water are simple to cross. The drivers merely make bridges of their own bodies, allowing the other ants to pass over them to the opposite bank.

Why do army ants march? What makes them stop and camp? Scientists used to think it was only the search for food. Now they believe it is the reproductive cycle as well. The ants march for approximately two weeks and rest for about three. They stop to let the queen lay her eggs and to allow the eggs to change into larvae. Meanwhile the

A queen of the primitive Ectatomma tuberculatum *ants closely resembles a worker.*

A large predatory Daceton *ant drags its prey over the ground.*

pupae, born at the previous stop, are struggling to break free of their cocoons. Their wriggling as they hatch into callow workers excites the ant colony. The colony breaks camp and moves on, carrying the new larvae.

Like the armies of men, the drivers have their followers. Certain species of wasps and beetles travel with the columns and help eat the meat of the victims. There are rear-guard soldiers too. Eyewitnesses have described "reserve" columns of army ant soldiers who carry on the attack after the front-rank soldiers have conquered a large number of victims. The reserve columns will march in one direction, toward the victims, while the front-rank columns go the other way carrying their spoils of meat.

When the ants stop marching, they form a living ball of ants with a hollow space in the center for the queen and the young. So completely organized are these ants that tunnels are formed by the bodies of the soldiers to permit ants passage to the central spaces.

Slave-Making Ants

The army ants of the tropics march to find food, but the sanguinary ants march for other reasons. Sanguinary means bloodthirsty, or cruel, and these ants are slave raiders. There are many types of slave raider ants, even in our own country, such as the northeastern bloodred ants with brown or black abdomens. These ants prey on more peaceful kinds of black ants, whose nests they rob of their pupae. The sanguinary ants take the pupae back to their own nests, and raise them. The captive ants will take over much of the work in the nest when they become adults.

Amazon ants, named after a tribe of women warriors who fought against the Greeks, are found both in Europe and America. In many ways, they are the

The Odontomachus *ant of the Solomon Islands has enormous jaws.*

most unusual slave raiders of all. The Amazons have jaws shaped like curved icepicks. Such a pair of jaws can easily pierce the armor of a smaller ant. But if the jaws are weapons of war, they are useless for breaking up food and doing domestic work in the nest. Therefore, the Amazons have become parasites, animals which must depend on other animals to help them live. The Amazons must capture other ants and make slaves of them; otherwise the Amazons would not be able to take care of themselves.

Since the bodies of the Amazons are so completely designed for warfare that they cannot even bring up their own young, the new Amazon queen must

This giant queen is an inch long.

begin her colony by forcing her way into the queen chamber of the gray *Formica* ant. There, she gathers together the pupae of the host ant and fights off attacks of the workers. Eventually, the Amazon queen murders the host queen and takes her place. She is accepted and adopted by the *Formica* workers who will spend their lives bringing up Amazon offspring.

Of course, after the death of the gray queen, no new gray ants can be born. The Amazons begin to outnumber the grays, and eventually new slaves are needed. The Amazons send out scouts to discover new gray nests. Then, when a new nest is found, though it may be hundreds of feet away, the Amazons group together and march to war. The gray ants defend their nest bravely, but the Amazons are bigger and faster. Also, the short, dull jaws of the grays are no match for the sharp jaws of the Amazons. In a day or so, the Amazons have killed many gray ants and returned to the original nest with a fresh supply of young gray ant cocoons. These cocoons become worker gray ants which immediately become slaves to the Amazons. When the young Amazon queens leave the nest to start new colonies, the cycle repeats itself.

The jaws of the Odontomachus *overlap each other when they are closed.*

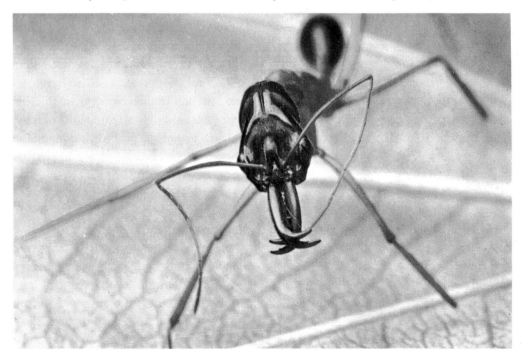

Harvester ants collect grain and grass seed.

Farmer Ants

Nowhere in the animal kingdom are there farmers to match the ants. Ants reap grain, grow fungus, and milk aphid "cows" for their honeydew. Through their social instincts the ants have learned secrets of agriculture far beyond the understanding of any other animal.

GRAIN HARVESTERS

The harvester ants, of the genus *Messor,* are found in many parts of the world. Sometimes smooth little highways, like the spokes of a wheel, can be seen running through grain fields. These tiny highways come together at the mound entrances of the harvester ants. Worker ants collect grains and grass seeds. They carry the grain along the highways, then scurry underground into tunnels and storerooms where the grain and seeds are stored until they are eaten.

Around the mounds of the harvester ants, patches of grass may grow thickly. It was once thought that the ants planted their own seeds to provide a convenient source of food, but it is more likely that seeds were merely dropped by ants on the way into the nest.

LEAFCUTTERS

More advanced than the harvester ants are the leaf-cutting ants of the tropics, the *Atta* ants from Central and South America. These ants swarm into trees and out onto the branches. They move their jaws like scissors and chew

A fungus garden is cultivated by leafcutters.

A leafcutter ant carries a leaf overhead.

off small pieces from the leaves. The *Attas* are known as "parasol" ants because each ant carries its piece of leaf above its head like a parasol. The leaf particles are taken underground where they are chewed into pulpy bits by other worker ants. The *Attas* do not eat the leaves; they use them as mulch to grow a special type of fungus. When the fungus begins to grow, the ants bite off the little fungus heads that form.

The *Attas* actually weed their gar-

Leafcutters cut and gather leaves from which they grow fungus.

Aphids are "milked" by the ants for their honeydew.

dens, to make sure that only their own type of fungus is allowed to grow. Adult ants live on the fungus, and their larvae are placed in the gardens so that abundant food will surround them all the time. The leafcutters are very independent. No matter what the weather, no matter what the season, they can always make the fungus grow underground. The leafcutters breed in large numbers, and a single nesting area may cover a hundred or more square yards. The entrance holes to the mounds may be three or four inches wide, and the depth of the tunnels over twenty feet. The underground fungus gardens are enormous. Some rooms may be three feet long and a foot wide. The ants must be careful to control their fungus garden. If it is too large, untended fungi will spread and crowd out the ant colony.

APHID TENDERS

Many kinds of ants tend aphids. Aphids, or plant lice, are tiny green insects which cluster on plants. They have long sucking tubes with which they pierce plant stems in order to draw out sap. Ants are fond of honeydew, which aphids get from the sap; when aphids are stroked by ant antennae, they squeeze out a drop of honeydew from their abdomens, and the ants lap it up. Ants protect their aphid "cattle," sometimes building leaf or wood pulp walls (known as "cartons") around them while they are clustered on plants. If other insects in search of honey or aphid meat come too close to the aphids, the ants drive them away by attacking with their jaws and poison.

The cornfield ants are expert aphid tenders. These ants live below the roots

38

of cornstalks and their aphid cattle never see the sunshine. The eggs of aphid mothers are cared for by the ants, and when the aphids grow to adults they begin drawing juices from the cornstalk roots. Cornfield ants depend largely upon aphid honeydew for their food, and many generations of aphids live under these ant masters.

HONEY ANTS

Aphids are not the only source of honeydew for the ants. Cactus plants in the desert provide sweet juices, as do many other plants.

Sometimes oak galls, or swellings on oak tree branches, are covered with crystal droplets of honeydew. A certain type of tiny, wasp-like insect lays her egg in the soft green stem of an oak tree branch. A swelling grows on the branch as the wasp larva increases in size.

Honeydew sap oozes out of this gall, and the ants drink the liquid.

Ants eat yet another kind of honeydew which drips from swollen female coccids, or scale insects. These round insects occur commonly on oaks and are sometimes mistaken for true oak galls, which they closely resemble.

In the Southwest and other dry regions desert ants use their own workers as living storage pots for honey. First, worker ants gather honey in their crops, or social stomachs, and return to the nest. Then, in special underground rooms, the storage pot ants, called repletes, cling to the ceiling and allow themselves to be filled with honey. These ants, patiently clinging to the dirt ceilings, act as storage pots all their lives. The repletes give up their honey to other workers of the colony when they are stroked by ant antennae.

Ants gather honeydew from a female coccid.

A honey ant stores honeydew in its abdomen.

Parasites

Ants do not always live alone in their nests. Nests broken open may reveal a strange assortment of dwellers. Besides ants, there may be caterpillars, grubs, cockroaches, and worms. The nest may also contain large numbers of aphids and beetle guests. These visitors are known as parasites. Some are welcome and some are unwelcome.

BEETLE GUESTS

Most beetle guests are welcome. There are over one thousand kinds of beetles that live with the ants. One of the most interesting is the clavigerid beetle, which begs for food by stroking ants with its antennae in much the same way the ants stroke each other. The ants pump up food for the beetles, and in return, the beetles have something to offer, too. On their backs are clumps of hair. When the hairs are stroked, glands secrete an intoxicating sweetish liquid which the ants greedily lap up.

Lomechusa beetles are frequent guests of the ants. Unfortunately for the ants, the lomechusa beetles lay eggs in the nest, and when the eggs change into larvae, they feed on ant eggs and receive precious food from ant nursemaids. The beetle larvae resemble ant larvae and the ants do not seem to notice the dif-

Ants stroke the back of a paussid beetle to obtain a sweet liquid.

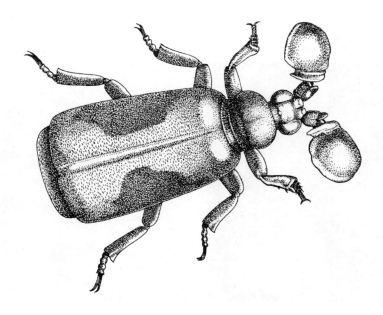

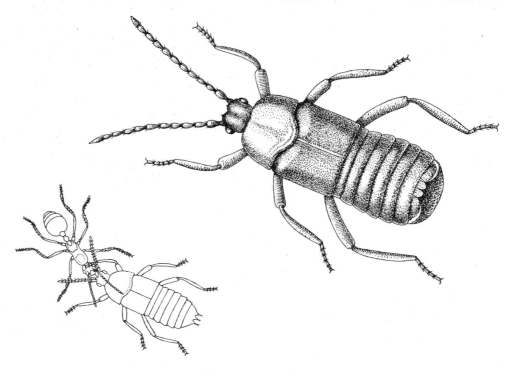

The lomechusa beetle is a dangerous enemy of an ant colony.

ference. When an ant nest is attacked the lomechusa larvae and pupae will be carried to safety before the ant larvae and pupae.

Besides the lomechusas, there are other types of beetles whose larvae feed on ant young, and of course, an ant population can be in danger of dwindling away. When this happens, the adult beetles crawl out of the nest, fly away, and search for new ant nests in which to live and lay their eggs.

The little cockroach under the ant makes its home in Atta *colonies.*

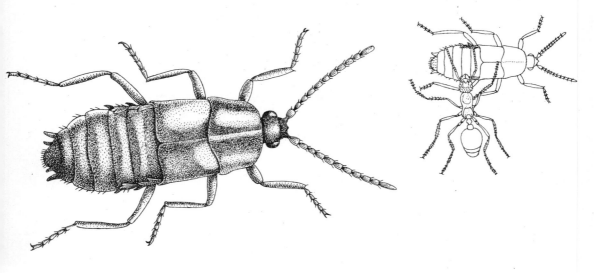

The atemeles beetle is another insect that inhabits ant nests.

UNWELCOME GUESTS

Unwelcome parasites, when discovered by the ants, are usually driven out. But some, like the dinarda beetles, are so well protected by their hard shells that the ants cannot successfully attack them. These insects are safe, and they continue to plunder the ant nests.

Small parasite insects, such as lepismatids hide in ant tunnels and rush out when two ants stop to feed each other. Just as a drop of liquid passes from one ant mouth to another, the lepismatids robber scurries between the ants and steals the food from their jaws.

Another parasite is the tiny thief ant, which feeds on the young of larger ants. Thief ants build their nests very close to the tunnels of a colony made of larger ants. Then they rush out of their narrow tunnels and make quick raids into the nurseries and food storage rooms. The larger ants chase them, but the thief ants discharge an unpleasant odor which successfully repels their pursuers.

Tiny thief ants will eat the food, the wastes and the young of larger ant colonies.

Some Ants Are Pests

Fortunately, northern countries do not suffer as much as tropical countries from damage caused by ants. The South American *Attas* can strip trees and bushes of their leaves in a single night, and army ants can kill and eat domestic animals as large as rabbits. Northern ants are usually smaller in size, fewer in number, and far less fierce than their southern cousins. Still, every year in the United States, ants are responsible for millions of dollars worth of damage, especially to crops.

Ant predators strip a plant.

Ants may be imported on shiploads of food from other countries.

IMPORTED ANTS

Many ant pests in the United States have been imported accidentally. Most of these ants are native to tropical regions, such as the forests of Central and South America, and the tiny pharaoh ant comes from as far away as Africa. Ants arrive in bundles of food and fabrics transported in the holds of ships, and if conditions are favorable in the new country, they begin to multiply, sometimes replacing or driving out local species. Trains and trucks with bundles of merchandise help carry ant colonies into different states.

THE ARGENTINE ANTS

No foreign ants have multiplied so rapidly and easily as the Argentines. Argentines were imported from South America near the beginning of the century, most likely aboard coffee ships from Brazil. Today, they are found in households and on farms from the Pacific to the Atlantic coast. They are hardy ants, and their feeding habits include almost every type of food. Argentines nest not only in the ground, but in woodpiles, house foundations, and even in old tin cans. The Argentines are the most injurious of all ant species in this

If their nest is disturbed, fire ants rush out fiercely to sting the invader.

Imported Argentine ants

country. They ruin gardens and orchards, and occasionally invade houses in such great numbers that the houses must be vacated.

THE FIRE ANTS

Another imported ant, the fire ant, causes trouble in the South. These ants, like the Argentines, are also native to South America, and probably arrived in the United States around 1920. Fire ants were first seen in Alabama, and are now found in ten states ranging from Texas to South Carolina. They are reddish-brown and their name comes from their fiery sting. They sting by gripping the flesh with their jaws and plunging

The mounds of the imported fire ant have ruined pastureland and crops.

their stingers into the wound. The sting is painful to human beings, and may cause death to small animals. Fire ants do damage to valuable crops by gnawing holes in roots and stalks, but more annoying to farmers are their hard dirt mounds. These dome-shaped mounds may be over a foot high, and there may be more than a hundred mounds in one acre of farmland. Blades of harvesting machines strike the mounds and become twisted, and workers in the fields are in constant danger of being stung by ants swarming out to defend their nests.

HOUSEHOLD PESTS

Other ant pests include the tiny pavement ant, the red pharaoh ant, the little black ant, and various types of garden ant. The insect exterminator, with his

Little black ants

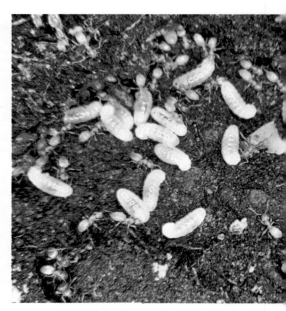

Yellow lawn ant

Odorous house ant

Acrobatic ant

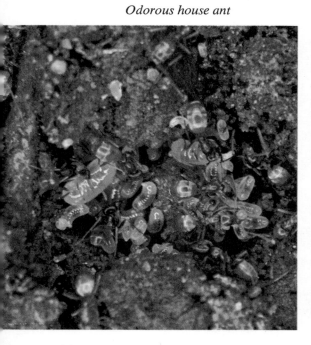

Termites are pale in color and are not true ants.

knowledge of ant colonies, can usually keep these minor pests under control. Most ant poisons work this way: The worker ants drink the poison and carry the liquid back to the nest in their crops. Thus, the worker ants unknowingly poison the queens and the young ants that have remained at home.

TERMITES

Termites are not true ants, though many people call them "white ants." Like the ant, the termite has only two body sections, although the thorax of the termite is not so clearly separated from the abdomen. Most ants are shiny and dark in color, but termites are soft and pale. In matters of colony life, the termites differ also from the ants. Worker ants are all wingless females, but workers in a termite colony may be either male or female.

Termites live underground, but they chew upwards into wood, eating out long passages in the direction of the wood grain. Termites actually eat wood, and do not spit out the sawdust as carpenter ants do. In order to digest wood, termite stomachs contain tiny, one-celled animals called protozoa. Protozoa change the cellulose of the wood into digestible, animal food.

Sometimes the foundations of houses are so weakened by termites that the buildings must be torn down, or foundation lumber replaced. Termites dislike light, and they build thin tubes of mud or wood pulp so they can climb from the ground to the wood in sealed passages. Since the destructive work of termites cannot be seen easily, wooden foundations should be checked periodically for termite damage.

Termites have some friends and many enemies in the ant world. Friendly ants lives as the termites' guests and will help defend the nest against invaders. Other ants, like the *Odontomachus* and species of *Ponerinae*, eat termites as a staple food and raid termite nests regularly.

Termites build tubes of wood cemented with saliva to keep out light, which they dislike.

A slice downwards through an ant nest reveals a busy city.

Watching Ants

Watching the ants at work can be a fascinating pastime. Ants are so common that it is not difficult to find an ant mound, or a "front door" in the ground, or a nest under a stone. Most types of ground-dwelling ants are easy to watch, and their holes can be found by following ants returning with food to the nest.

If some food, such as sugar mixed with water or a freshly killed insect, is placed near an ant nest, the ants will discover it quickly and surround it. A magnifying glass will show how the workers tear the food apart and carry it home to the nest. It will also show the enlargement of the abdomen as an ant fills its crop with liquid. Some observers have learned to mark the bodies of worker ants with a touch of paint on the end of a single strand of brush. Such markings prove that the same ants make repeated trips between food sources and the nest.

ANTS IN ARTIFICIAL NESTS

Ants like the Argentines perform interesting nest building below ground, and therefore a viewing-box is helpful.

49

Ants' activities can be observed in this commercial "ant farm."

A viewing-box enables the observer to study the ants' underground activities as if a cross section were cut through an ordinary nest. Viewing-boxes can be as simple as two panes of glass held in a wood frame, or more elaborate, with feeding stations and a water moat. A separate feeding station lets the ants eat as much as they need and no leftover food remains to soil the nest.

The best way to collect ants like the Argentines is to place the viewing-box, filled with moist dirt, on top of the entrance hole to a ground nest. If food is placed between the glass panes, and the top left open, the ants will soon form a scent trail in and out of the box. Then, after eight hours or so, a gentle flooding

of the ground with a garden hose will force the ants from their nest and into the dry protection of the box. So strong is the building instinct, that the first workers to arrive will begin at once to carve new rooms and tunnels. Flooding should stop when worker ants begin carrying eggs, larvae, and pupae into the box, and also after several queens have found their way inside. If the box is placed in a moat of shallow water, the ants will not escape.

The best time for ant collecting is spring or early summer. This is the time for egg laying and nest building. In very cold months, and throughout the winter, ants are not very active, and some members of the colony hibernate. A colony gathered in the spring should reveal the stages of growth from egg to adult.

An open viewing-box is best for experiments in ant feeding, since the workers can leave the box. A thin stick of wood leading from the top of the glass to a food supply will provide a study of how rapidly ants search and find food. If the stick is turned upside down, or moved slightly to a new position, the ants will be confused until a new scent trail is established.

Since ants build toward the darkness, not the light, it is necessary to make covers of dark cardboard for the viewer. If the panes of glass are not covered, ants will build their tunnels and rooms deep in the dirt, out of sight. The cardboard can be lifted for observation periods. It should not be lifted too frequently, for repeated changes from light to darkness disturbs the ordinary life of the ant colony more than longer periods of light.

Feeding stations may be set in water to prevent ants from escaping.

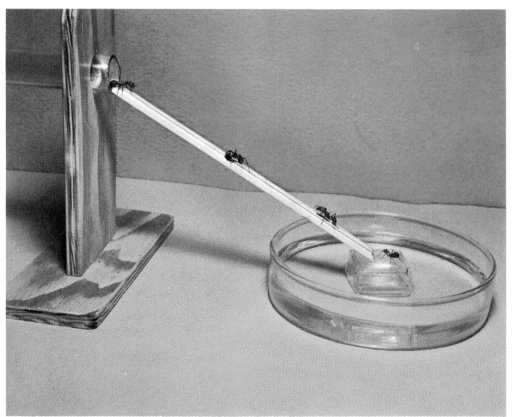

Members of the Ant Family

The scientific family name for all ants is *Formicidae*. There are over 6,000 known species of ants, with several hundred more being discovered and identified each year. Among the ant species there are both more social and less social members, the latter being found chiefly among the most primitive kinds of ants, and the more social ones being also the most highly developed species. Ants range in length from 1/25 of an inch to two inches and all are grouped into eight sub-families, listed below:

SUB-FAMILY and Characteristic

PONERINAE
  Most primitive
CERAPACHYINAE
  Next most primitive
DORYLINAE
  Army ants of India, Africa, and
  South America
MYRMICINAE
  Largest and most diverse of the
  sub-families
LEPTANILLINAE
  Microscopic army ants
PSUEDOMYRMINAE
  Rare, thin species, which lives be-
  tween the bark and trunks of trees
DOLICHODERINAE
  Fast scavenger ants
FORMICINAE
  Most highly developed of the species

Formica *ant dragging a bee*

52

Bottle-tailed ant

Harvester ant and berry

TABLE OF ILLUSTRATED ANTS

SUB-FAMILY	COMMON NAME	SCIENTIFIC NAME
PONERINAE	Keleps, bulldog ants	*Odontomachus,* 34, 35
	Guatemalan kelep	*Ectatomma tuberculatum,* 32
DORYLINAE	Army ants, driver ants, 19, 23, 31, 32	*Dorylus* (Africa) *Eciton* (Central, S. America), 9
MYRMICINAE	Fire ants, 9, 17, 20, 26, 44, 45	*Solenopsis geminata*
	Harvester ants, 7, 36, 42	*Phelidole, Messor, Pogonomyrmex,* 35
	Leafcutters, 16, 37	*Atta,* 9, 29, 41
	Pharaoh ant, 45	*Monomorium pharaonis*
DOLICHODERINAE	Argentine ant, 45	*Iridomyrmex humilis*
	Odorous house ant, 46	*Tapinoma sessile*
FORMICINAE	Carpenter ants, 4, 8, 18, 21, 24, 25	*Camponotus*
	Janitor ants	*Colobopsis,* 27
	Spiny tree ant	*Polyrhachis,* 28
	Honey ants, 39	*Myrmecocystus*
	Amazon, robber ant, 34	*Polyergus rufescens*
	Sanguinary ant	*Formica sanguinea*
	Wood, hill, red, horse ants, 7, 11, 26	*Formica rufa*
	Gray ant, 5, 54	*Formica fusca,* 12, 52
	Green tree, weaver ants, 28	*Oecophylla*
	Cornfield ant	*Lasius americanus*
	Yellow lawn ant, 46	*Acanthomyops*

Index

abdomen, 7, 12
acrobatic ant, 46
Amazon ants, 34, 35
ant collecting, 50
antenna, 10, 30, 38, 39
aphids, 10, 38, 39
Argentine ants, 22, 29, 30, 44, 50
army ants, 31-33
artificial nests, 49-51
Atta ants, 29, 36-38, 43

beetles, 40-42
   clavigerid, 40
   dinarda, 42
   lomechusa, 40, 41
   paussid, 40
blood, 11
bottle-tailed ants, 52

callow, 21, 25
carpenter ants, 26
Chilean desert ant, 29
chitin, 7
cockroach, 21, 41
cocoons, 27
colonies, 22-25
compound nests, 22
cornfield ants, 38, 39
crop, 12
crop damage, 44, 45

Daceton ant, 9, 33
dinosaur, 14
drivers, 9, 31, 32
drones, 23

Eciton, 9, 31

eggs, 18, 19, 22, 24, 25
eyes, 9

fire ants (imported), 45
   mounds, 26, 45
flower-ball homes, 27, 28
food, 7, 10, 11, 12, 36, 37, 40
Formica, 35
Formicinae, 30
fungus, 37, 38

gray ants, 35

harvester ants, 36
head, 7, 9, 10
homes, 22, 26-29, 40, 49
honeydew, 12, 38, 39
Hymenoptera, 8
imported ants, 43-45
instinct, 15, 16, 21

janitor ant, 26, 27
jaws, 9, 30, 34, 35

larva, 17, 19, 20, 25, 28
leafcutters, 36-38
lepismatids, 42
little black ants, 26, 46

mandibles (jaws), 7, 11
Messor, 36
monarch butterfly, 17
mud-ball home, 27

nests (*see* homes)

oak gall, 39

Odontomachus ant, 48
odor trail, 10
odorous house ant, 46

parasites, 40-42
pavement ant, 45
pharaoh ant, 44, 45
poison, 12, 30
Ponerinae, 48
prehistoric ants, 13-15
   bird, 13
   horse, 13
pupa, 17, 20, 21, 24, 31

queen, 22-25, 32

replete, 39

saliva, 11, 25
sanguinary ants, 34
scent trail, 10
silverfish, 42
slave-making ants, 34
stingers, 12
stomach (*see* abdomen)
swarming, 23, 24

termites, 47, 48
thief ant, 42
thorax, 7, 11, 25

viewing box, 49-51

wars, 30
weaver ants, 28, 29
wings, 11
wood ants, 26, 27, 30
workers, 21, 25, 26, 36

PICTURE CREDITS. *American Museum of Natural History,* pp. 32 (top), 49; W. A. Pluemer, p. 19 (top); James E. Thompson, p. 19 (bot. l.). John W. Green, p. 26 (bot.). Ross E. Hutchins, pp. 6, 9 (top r. & bot. l.), 10, 16, 17 (bot.), 20 (top), 25, 26 (top l.), 27, 28, 34 (top), 35, 37 (top l.), 39 (r.), 41, 42 (bot.), 45 (top), 46 (bot.), 48, 50, 51. *Monkmeyer Press Photo Service,* Alexander B. Klots, p. 38 (r.); E. S. Ross, pp. 9 (top l. & bot. r.), 12, 29, 31, 33, 37 (top r. & bot.), 38 (l.), 52 (ctr. & bot.). *National Audubon Society,* Lynwood M. Chace, p. 24 (bot.); Stephen Collins, p. 17 (top r.); Fran Hall, p. 39 (l.); William J. Jahoda, p. 24 (top); Billy Jones, p. 52 (top); Harold Peters, p. 45 (bot.); S. J. Swanne, p. 17 (top l.); Grace A. Thompson, cover, pp. 8, 18 (top), 21, 22, 36, 44. T. C. Schneirla, pp. 19 (bot. r.), 23, 34 (bot.). *Shostal,* Robert Leahey, p. 43. Roman Vishniac, pp. 4, 8 (bot.), 20 (bot.), 26 (top r.), 30, 42 (top), 46 (top), 47. *Wide World,* p. 43.